16 Life Lessons from:

The Rock Tumbler

Own Your Journey!

Romans 8:37

16 Life Lessons from:

The Rock Tumbler

To Conquer The World By Becoming

Who You're Meant To Be

*How You View The World And, More Importantly, How
You Interact With The World Greatly Affects What You
Will Get Out Of The World.*

Chad Busick

XULON PRESS

Xulon Press
2301 Lucien Way #415
Maitland, FL 32751
407.339.4217
www.xulonpress.com

Illustrated by Alex Dieringer

Unless otherwise indicated, Scripture quotations taken
from the Holy Bible, New International Version (NIV).
Copyright © 1973, 1978, 1984, 2011 by Biblica, Inc.™.
Used by permission. All rights reserved.

Paperback ISBN-13: 978-1-6322-1408-9

Hard Cover ISBN-13: 978-1-6322-1409-6
Ebook ISBN-13: 978-1-6322-1410-2

To my wife, Jennifer, and my daughters,
Shayne and Morgan:
you inspire me to be a better husband and father.

Contents

Foreword

Every once in a while a person comes across your path that you 'click' with. I met Chad in a class I was giving some 25 years ago. His response to the concepts I used in my class and the technique I used to facilitate the concepts resonated with him. Ever since then, he has been not only a good friend to me but he has also inspired me.

His dedication to making a positive difference in the world shows in the story of the rocks. In this book, he has captured what it takes to "take a licking and keep on ticking" to achieve our goals. Chad's way of comparing the life of a rock to our lives, especially during times of uncertainty and change, shows us that if we have a vision, persistence, and drive, we can push through the rough times, stay focused on our dreams, vision and passion, and we can persevere.

Chad has done a masterful job in creating an example of the significance of personal vision, illustrated by The Rock Tumbler, and what one has to go through to conquer their goals. Life is not easy, we have all taken mental hits, but if you stick with it you will come out of it like the rocks in this story--shiny and smooth.

Jim Madrid
CEO and Founder
Advance Sports Technology

I

Chip And Corey

I first met Chip and Corey while I was out on a run one day. Taking a break from my busy schedule, the run gave me some much-needed time away from the demands of work, family, and life. It was an opportunity to gather my thoughts, clear my mind and connect with nature. Over the past few years, I had probably run this same three-mile loop hundreds of times, but that day, something was different. As I began my run, I started to notice things around me. First, I noticed a new car on our street, then a few birds feasting on some trash left on the sidewalk. Next, I saw a couple butterflies fluttering around some flowers as a hummingbird buzzed by in search of his next meal. I turned off the road and onto the trail. Cutting through the trees, a squirrel darted across the path, scrambling up the nearest tree.

As I turned the corner, I ran into Chip and Corey. I had crossed over this same section of the trail so many times and had never noticed them before. Stopping quickly, I bent down for a closer look. It was evident to me that they had been there for quite a while. I reached down,

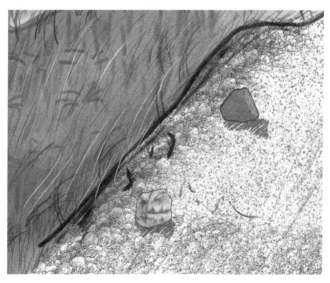

picked them up, and continued my run. When I got home, I examined my new rocks a little more closely. While I found them together and in the same environment, there was something different about each of them. I began to wonder where they had come from and what they had been through. Both of them were unique in their own way.

With the addition of Chip and Corey, my rock collection was complete, and it was time to get out my rock tumbler. As I placed the rocks in the tumbler, I began to think about Chip and Corey. Like many people in the world, Chip was concerned about fitting in within his new environment. His identity had always been tied to his performance and his results. While Chip had enjoyed previous success in life, he often tied his worth to what others thought of him. Constantly on the lookout for any possible threats, Chip was focused on every interaction, as he thought each interaction either supported or challenged who he was.

On the other hand, there was something different about Corey. He had a calmness about him. Unlike Chip, Corey wasn't nervous about fitting in. It was clear that Corey's identity was in something completely different. He seemed to understand exactly who he was, which always allowed him to have a clearer focus. While the results and being successful were certainly important to Corey, he focused his attention on the process of becoming better.

As I closed the rock tumbler, I couldn't help but wonder what would happen over the next few weeks. I plugged in the tumbler, and it began to rotate. Round and round it went. The minutes turned to hours, the hours turned to days, and the days turned to weeks until it was time to remove the rocks for the last time. I opened the tumbler and began my search for Chip and Corey...

II

The Tumbler

When rocks go into the rock tumbler, one of two things will result from this process. Some rocks will be ground down and ultimately reduced to almost nothing; others will be reshaped and redefined into glorious, beautiful rocks—an unlikely transformation from the beginning of the process. Looking at these rocks when they enter the rock tumbler, we could never imagine what their results would be.

The world we live in is like a big rock tumbler. How we view the world, interact with the world, and respond to the world has a huge impact on the people we become. Like rocks in the rock tumbler, we can either be ground down and reduced to only a fraction of ourselves or see our circumstances as a way to mold us and shape us into the people we are meant to be. The big difference is that, unlike rocks, we get to have a say in how we view and interact with these circumstances.

As we move forward, we will take a closer look at the following ABC's of the rock tumbler: A) The Ingredients, B) The Process, and C) The Results. Along the way, we will identify sixteen life lessons from the rock tumbler. Next, we will revisit our friends Chip and Corey before I share some final thoughts. We will then finish up with taking a closer look at the sixteen lessons – Beyond *The Rock Tumbler*. **Ready, set, let's tumble…**

Part A—The Ingredients

Lesson #1 – Your Rock

As we begin our journey through the rock tumbler, we will need to gather the four ingredients that will be going into the tumbler. The first ingredient needed is your rock. Your rock represents not only who you are but what you have been through. In today's world, it is so easy to become distracted. We are constantly pulled in various directions, and as authors Brad Stulberg and Steve Magness share in their must-read book, *The Passion Paradox*, "What is important doesn't necessarily get our attention; what gets our attention becomes important…whatever attracts our attention is king" (2019, 102).

It has been said that time is our most valuable resource. While our time is certainly valuable and something that we never seem to have enough of, our most precious resource is our undivided attention. In a world with constant battles for our attention, very little actually gets our full, undivided attention. In fact, we often celebrate our ability to multi-task even though, as author Simon Sinek puts it in his book, *Leaders Eat Last:*

> The evidence is indisputable. Despite what they or anyone believes, with rare exceptions, those who think they are more productive because they are better at multitasking are just wrong. What they are better at is being distracted. (2017, 257)

As we transition into the remaining lessons from the rock tumbler, it is important that we understand that showing up and truly being present is the most valuable thing that we can do. So much about what we get out of life has everything to do with what we put into it. Without showing up and being present in life, growth is impossible. The rock tumbler asks us to bring our true and complete self into the arena, whether that be in our jobs, in our relationships, or in any other aspect of our lives.

Lesson #2 – The Other Rocks

Our world is filled with other rocks, or other people. The people in our lives come in all sorts of shapes and sizes. Some have large roles in our lives while others play smaller roles. There are people we are happy to have in the tumbler with us, whether that be family, close friends, or anyone else that we enjoy doing life with. On the other hand, there are people that we would probably throw out of the tumbler if we were given the choice. Everyone with whom we come in contact has an opportunity to help shape us into the people we are becoming. Some people who have a positive impact on our lives help push us forward by teaching us who we want to be. Others may leave marks on us, taking parts of us with them as they leave us hurt or broken while teaching us who we don't want to be.

Unfortunately, these negative interactions often have the biggest impact on our lives. Whether we are scarred by an absent parent, an abusive relationship, the loss of a loved one, or any other of the countless circumstances that can leave us physically, mentally, or emotionally wounded, we have the opportunity to move through those moments by carrying those scars but still pressing on toward who we are to become. Just because we aren't the people we want to be or in the place we want to be doesn't mean that we can't end up there. The rocks in the tumbler don't second guess themselves or wonder why the tumbling is happening—instead, they keep moving forward toward the final goal.

Lesson #3 – Grit

In addition to adding rocks of various sizes to the tumbler, we must add a couple more things. The first thing we need to add is grit. Honestly, I can't make this up. For the rock tumbler, grit is a sand-like or gravel-like substance that helps shape and mold the rocks. During the initial stage, a coarser or rougher grit is needed to break-down the rocks. Throughout the process, the grit that is added transitions from coarse to medium to fine. Grit is what gets into the cracks and crevices to keep us going, and it helps reduce the friction the other rocks have caused. As goes the rock tumbler, so goes life, and like rocks, we also need grit in our lives. In addition to grit being a material substance, Merriam-Webster defines grit as "firmness of mind or spirit: unyielding courage in the face of hardship or danger" (2020). Grit encourages us to keep going even when things are stacked against us. Grit seems to know that there are better days and better things to come. Angela Duckworth, author of *Grit: The Power of Passion and Perseverance (2016),* has dedicated much of her career to studying grit. According to Duckworth, "Grit is passion and persistence applied toward long-term achievement, with no particular concern for rewards or recognition along the way" (Fessler 2018). Whether it's in the rock tumbler or in our lives, grit plays an important role, not only in the process but also in the results.

Lesson #4 – Water

The final ingredient to add to the rock tumbler is water. The water plays an important role inside the tumbler, as it helps the other ingredients do their job. Without the water, the grit would be unable to flow in and around the rocks. The water also helps to soften the impact of the rocks as they tumble. This addition of water can be viewed as either overwhelming or life giving. Thankfully, the rocks don't overthink this process; otherwise, they might believe they were drowning. Enough water is added to the tumbler to just about cover the rocks. Unfortunately, so many people in the world today feel like they are just one drop of water away from going under. They think that if just one more thing happens or something else is added to their situation, they won't be able to make it out.

Even though this can seem overwhelming, when you begin to feel this way, keep moving forward. We should be looking at the water as life giving, for it helps to sustain us and provides the foundation for our future growth. Who is it that is pouring into you? In your life, who provides the much-needed nutrients to encourage you and lift you up when you need it most? And importantly, who are the people, whether family or friends, you are pouring into?

Part B—The Process

Lesson #5 – Let's Get Ready to Tumble

After the rocks, grit, and water have been added to the barrel of the rock tumbler, it's time to close the lid. Once closed tightly, the barrel is placed onto the rotating shafts of the rock tumbler, where it begins to tumble. For the next seven days, the tumbler will continue to spin. Round and round it goes, over and over again, without stopping. For many people, life seems to be a never-ending cycle where they can never seem to catch up. It's easy to compare the rock tumbler to the hamster wheel of life. Real progress happens by staying focused on the present instead of trying to look ahead for the end result or behind to see where you have been. At some level, we all understand that growth and improvement take work, which takes time.

Lesson #6 – Taking a Break

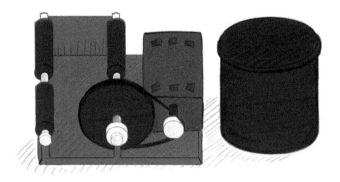

After seven days, or 168 hours, in the rock tumbler, it is time to take the rocks out of the tumbler. This part of the process also teaches us another valuable lesson. In order to become the people we are meant to be, we sometimes need to take a break. We can't simply remain in the same spin cycle forever. Once again, as with the rock tumbler, we need to know when to hit the stop button. In fact, rest is an important component of growth and improvement. According to Stulberg and Magness, the secret to growth of "any muscle, be it physical, cognitive, or emotional—is balancing the right amount of stress with the right amount of rest. Stress + rest = growth. This equation holds true regardless of what it is that you are trying to grow" (2017, 28).

The challenge is that we often struggle with prioritizing rest. The world often conditions us to believe that if we rest or take a break, we will be falling behind, and the only way to keep up or get ahead is to keep going, regardless of the consequences. It is important that we find breaks within our own rock tumblers. Whether it be spending quality time with a spouse, attending a sporting event or a performance with the children, connecting with a friend, or setting aside time to work out, these important moments can provide much-needed breaks. We need to understand that by taking a break and resting, we can put ourselves in the best position for continued growth when we re-enter the arena.

Lesson #7 – Life Is Messy

Once the tumbling stops, the lid is removed, and what is revealed looks nothing like it did at the beginning. Underneath the lid is a dirty, muddy mess. In fact, you can hardly even see the rocks below the surface. Well, guess what? Just like the rock tumbler, life can be and often is messy. The effects of the world can leave us covered in mud, desperately grasping as we find ourselves under the weight of our circumstances. In life, we often discover that things tend to get worse before they get better. When we put ourselves into the arena, there will undoubtedly be roadblocks, setbacks, dead ends, speed bumps, hurdles, and obstacles, among any other analogy of the muddy mess that life can be. As author Ryan Holiday states in his book, *The Obstacle Is the Way,*

> You will come across obstacles in life—fair and unfair. And you will discover, time and time again, that what matters most is not what these obstacles are but how we see them, how we react to them, and whether we keep our composure. You will learn that this reaction determines how successful we will be in overcoming—or possibly thriving because of—them. (2014, 17)

What happens next and, more importantly, how we respond to these obstacles and challenges will have a huge impact on our future growth. Often, we can get stuck in the mud where our current situations paralyze us—holding us in the situations that we so badly want to escape.

Lesson #8 – Pulled out of the Mess

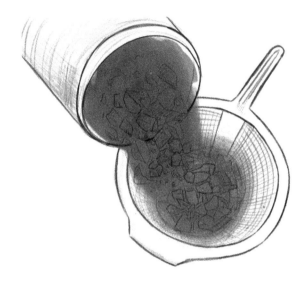

To move forward, the rocks need to be removed from the tumbler. One by one, the rocks are pulled out of the mess. Sometimes we have to get out of the mud before we can move forward. Whether others help us while we are being pulled out of the mess or after we are pulled out, a common theme seems to emerge over and over again. Most of the time, being removed from the mess requires us to depend on outside forces to help us. This help could come from a family member, close friend, mentor, counselor, pastor, or coach. It could also be our faith and dependence on a higher power. It is in these moments that we often find the powerful qualities of empathy and compassion. In his book *Conscious Coaching,* author Brett Bartholomew explains that "empathy and compassion involves the use of emotional payments when communicating. An emotional payment is when another individual actively and openly recognizes or validates the thoughts, concerns, and contributions of another in order to let them know they appreciate and understand them" (2017, 245).

During these times when we are often most vulnerable, having others meet us where we are and come along side us to invest these emotional payments can play a critical role in helping us move forward instead of remaining stuck in the mud. Who helps pull you out of the mess of life? When things get rough, who is there to pick you up? And just as important, who are you able to pull out of their mess?

Lesson #9 – Rinse

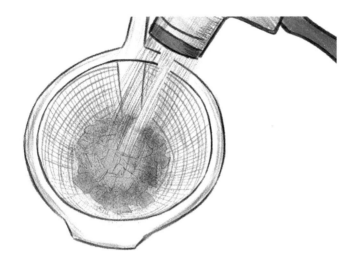

Once removed from the tumbler, the rocks are rinsed off to remove the mud and dirt, revealing growth and a revitalized sense of identity. Once again, the water is used to cleanse us. We need to rinse, recharge, and refresh before we can continue the process. What are the areas in your life that provide these much-needed moments? From little moments within a busy day to a nice dinner out, attending church on the weekend, or a vacation, these opportunities can provide what's necessary to keep us going.

One of the most powerful ways to rinse and refresh is through gratitude, which can actually help us combat stress. Jon Gordon, well known speaker and bestselling author of more than twenty books including *The Power of Positive Leadership*, shares that "the research shows that you can't be stressed and thankful at the same time" (2017, 96).

In other words, by practicing gratitude, we can help ourselves step away from the stress of life, which will prepare us to better handle what lies ahead. Want to take this to the next level? Consider adding a gratitude walk to your regular routine. Combining gratitude with exercise and nature can be a successful formula for helping us get away, recharge, and refresh. Think back to the beginning of this book and my discovery of Chip and Corey, which happened while I was running. In fact, much of the inspiration for the content and lessons for *The Rock Tumbler* came during my daily runs.

Lesson #10 – Deep Cleaning

After the rocks have been rinsed off, there will likely still be some mud and dirt left behind in the cracks and crevices. If not properly addressed, these leftover particles will have a negative impact on the next step in the process and even on the final results. Through careful examination, the rocks are scrubbed with a brush to ensure that the dirt and mud are completely removed.

Often, we see people get out of one situation only to jump right back into another one. In doing so, they are bringing with them additional baggage that affects their current and future situations. Similar to the rocks, scrubbing in our lives ensures that we will be ready to move forward as the best version of ourselves, while removing the additional weight that could hold us back from realizing our full potential. Author Brené Brown expands on this in her book, *Dare to Lead:*

> When we own our hard stories and rumble with them, we can write a new ending—an ending that includes how we're going to use what we've survived to be more compassionate and empathic. When we deny our stories of struggle, they own us. They own us, and they drive our behavior, emotions, thinking, and leading. Daring leadership is leading from heart, not hurt (2018, 114).

It's through the deep cleaning that we begin to own our stories. We need to understand that properly addressing these leftover particles at the right time gives us the opportunity to move forward effectively. Although definitely uncomfortable at the time, the long-term benefits will almost certainly outweigh the temporary pain associated with deeper self-reflection.

Lesson #11 – Repeat

At this point in the process, an interesting thing happens. If we are left outside of the arena for too long, we begin to dry up. In fact, when the rocks are removed from the tumbler, you want to keep them from drying out. That's right—even when taking a break from the tumbler, the rocks still need to stay connected to the process to prevent becoming stale. So, after being pulled out of the mud, rinsed off, and scrubbed clean, it's back into the tumbler. Then the entire process repeats—more days in the rock tumbler, more mess, and more mud, followed by being removed, rinsed off, scrubbed clean, and then placed back into the rock tumbler again. In life, this process repeats itself over and over again.

This is an important lesson, as the world today seems to be obsessed with the race to be the "best." Bestselling author Simon Sinek, in his recent book, *The Infinite Game* (2019), talks about the differences between having a finite mindset versus an infinite mindset. Sinek makes a compelling argument that while we are playing the infinite game of life, we often play according to finite rules. We can see this clearly in the world's desire to be the "best" instead of focusing on being "better." As Sinek points out,

> Infinite-minded leaders understand that "best" is not a permanent state. Instead, they strive to be "better." "Better" suggests a journey of constant improvement and makes us feel like we are being invited to contribute our talents and energies to make progress in that journey. "Better," in the Infinite Game, is better than "best" (57).

By re-entering the rock tumbler, we continue our journey—a journey that hopefully leads us to becoming the person we are meant to be.

Lesson #12 – The Process Summary

While the entire world is like a rock tumbler, we also experience areas or seasons of our lives in which we personally experience a rock-tumbler type of situation. Whether in our relationships, our occupations, or any other aspect of our lives, it seems that we consistently find ourselves either heading into a rock tumbler, in a rock tumbler, or coming out of a rock tumbler. The more we understand this, the better we will be prepared to not just accept the rock tumbler but even begin to embrace and appreciate the people we are becoming as of the result of the circumstances or situations within the rock tumbler. Given the amount of time that we will likely spend in the rock tumbler over the course of our lives, learning to focus on the process can be of great benefit to us. As we transition to the final part of *The Rock Tumbler*, the results, we will be taking a closer look at the difference between "the process" and "the results." To help us get there, consider the following quote from Stulberg and Magness: "Don't worry about being the best—worry about being the best at getting better" (2019, 88).

Part C – The Results

Lesson #13 – The Results Summary

The rock tumbler teaches us many important lessons; at the top of that list is the reminder that process is greater than results. The best results come when we are focused on the process. In the rock tumbler, the rocks are not worried about the end result but are fully committed to the process. For us, when we get things turned around, our results-driven world takes us away from focusing on the things that we need to excel at in order to make the results possible. In his bestselling book, *Atomic Habits (2018),* author James Clear explains the differences between focusing on goals or results and focusing on what he calls "systems," which concern the process by which we achieve our goals and results. He lays out four problems that focusing on goals can create in our lives. In the fourth problem, Clear contends that our goals can actually work against our long-term progress:

> The purpose of setting goals is to win the game. The purpose of building systems is to continue playing the game. True long-term thinking is goal-less thinking. It's not about any single accomplishment. It is about the cycle of endless refinement and continuous improvement. Ultimately, it is your commitment to the process that will determine your progress. (27)

Regardless of the results, no matter how great those results might be, the person you become (or don't become) in the process will be the ultimate measure of success. While the process can certainly be uncomfortable at times, it is through the process that the magic of growth and improvement happens.

Lesson #14 – Run Your Race

The rock tumbler also teaches that each of us are running our own races; this means my experiences are not your experiences and, therefore, my results will not be the same as your results. In the world today, we are often entangled by comparing ourselves to others. We have got to stop this comparison game, as our constant comparison often leads us to one of two things, and both of these outcomes are negative. At the extremes, the result of the comparisons can lead to pride or envy. When we compare ourselves to others in an area where we might come out on top, we must be careful that pride doesn't creep in undetected.

Pride can lead to many things including complacency, where we no longer measure our success against our own standards and can settle for simply being better than someone else. When this happens, we can let go of achieving our full potential by accepting something less. On the other hand, when we compare ourselves to others and come up short in that area, then we run the risk of feeling envy. When not handled correctly, envy can make several negative outcomes happen. Envy can lead us to becoming discouraged and even giving up on our dreams. In addition, it can cause us to focus on others, which takes us away from the talent and gifts that we have been given. Whether through pride or envy, the end result is that we stop living out our full potential and becoming the best version of ourselves. If we are unable to get away from these comparisons, we need to at least reframe the comparison into something that leads us to achieve our full potential. We should be comparing ourselves to our previous selves and our current selves to the future selves that we want to become. Are we better today than we were yesterday? Will we be better tomorrow than we are today?

This really comes down to what you choose to focus on. In the world today, thanks in large part to social media, there is a constant pull for us to put our focus onto what everyone else is doing. This often leads us right back to comparing our lives to what we see around us. Instead, we should be focusing on running our own race on our own path to the person we are becoming.

Lesson #15 – Appreciate the Grind

Like the rock tumbler, the world we live in will be a grind. We need to learn to accept and embrace the grind. There is going to be stress in our lives. In fact, trying to live a stress-free life is by nature stressful in itself. The purpose of the grind is not to accept or even buy into it, as those approaches tend to be passive. Instead, we need to change our mindset and "own the grind." Consider these words from Tim Tebow in his book, *This Is the Day*:

> There are areas in most of our lives where we can do better, reset our habits, or improve in some way. This will require us to dig deep, embrace the grind, and work hard. We may not be able to change our circumstances, but we can

learn and grow and develop our character from our experience. We don't have
to give up after failure; we can determine to find a way to make something
work. And that's the key word—work.
(2018, 125)

When we take ownership, we take an active role and commit the time and energy required for the grind to produce growth. We seem to have a common understanding that anything worth achieving in life will require at least some level of hard work. The challenge is to match the level of effort with the anticipated growth that we hope to achieve through the effort. Growth and improvement drive results.

Lesson #16 – You Are Meant to Shine

During the process, an interesting thing happens with the grit. While the amount of grit that is added remains the same, the type of grit changes at each stage of the process. At the beginning, the grit is much coarser and is designed to cut into and shape the rocks. Over time, however, the grit becomes less and less abrasive. This is true in our lives as well, as the beginning stages of the rock tumbler can be a real shock to our system. Yet, as we continue to grow and move through the rock tumbler, the grit no longer breaks us down; instead, it actually begins to refine us. In the final stage of the rock tumbler, the grit that is added is very fine and smooth. The purpose of this almost flour-like grit is to polish the rocks, which makes them shine. Just like the rocks, we too are not meant to merely survive the rock tumbler; rather, we are meant to shine as the people we have become.

III

Chip And Corey Revisited

As I rinsed off the rocks for the final time, I placed them on the table to dry. It was then that I noticed that something was missing. Over the course of the weeks of the rock tumbler's process, the tumbler had clearly taken its toll on Chip. The process of the rock tumbler had literally chipped away everything he had been. The first two times that I removed the rocks and cleaned them, it was evident that Chip was being worn down.

While searching for Chip, I began to think back to how much I had resembled him earlier in my life. There was a season of my life where I had a very successful career in sales. From the outside looking in, I had it all, including an excellent job, a million-dollar home, a second home, a boat, a loving wife, and two amazing daughters. So, what was the problem with that? I was living solely for my own interest. While I was succeeding in so many areas, there was still something missing. Unfortunately, I wouldn't realize what was missing until several years later.

On the other hand, Corey had different results from the rock tumbler. The tumbler had molded and shaped him into the best version of himself. By remaining true to his core identity, Corey was able to embrace the process that helped shape him. While Corey still had marks, blemishes, cracks, and other imperfections, they did not define who he was. Corey was rock solid in who he was, and because of that, he was willing to take the risks necessary in order to experience the growth and improvement that led to him becoming the best version of himself.

Once again, I found myself reflecting back on my life and how I want my life to resemble that of Corey. As a result of some external challenges, I found myself thrown back into the rock tumbler. The loss of my career led to big changes, including the loss of both of my houses. However, in the midst of the rock tumbler, I began to rediscover my true identity. I started to invest more time into my family, where I reconnected with my passion for coaching and my love for soccer. For the next ten years, I would spend countless hours at practice and on the sidelines with my daughters—time that I will forever be grateful for. As a family, we would spend weekends together traveling around to support them in their athletics.

During this time, I began to reconnect with my faith with renewed focus on my walk with the Lord. It was also during this time that I reconnected with my purpose. Since my senior year in high school, I always had a desire to work with players, coaches, and teams on the mental side of sports, and while in the rock tumbler, my desire and purpose began to come together. My past education, history in sales, and coaching experience opened up a new opportunity that ignited a spark that, when fanned with my newfound identity and purpose, led to tremendous growth. The rock tumbler had begun to shape and mold me into the person I am meant to be.

IV

Final Thoughts

Regardless of our position or role in life, it is impossible to avoid the rock tumbler. Whether in only certain areas of life or life as a whole, we will spend the majority of our lives either heading into, in the midst of, or on the way out of the rock tumbler. Instead of running from or trying to avoid the rock tumbler, perhaps we should try to change our relationship with it.

As previously stated, life is not about accepting or even embracing its challenges but rather "owning our journey." Far too many people are stuck in what has happened in the past, but our past doesn't have to define our present or determine our future or what we can become. In order to truly "own our journey," we need to start with two important truths. First of all, your circumstances, whether good or bad, do not define who you are or who you live for; however, how you respond to those circumstances will reveal who you are and who you live for. Secondly, when our identity is rock solid in who we are, the possibilities of what we can become are endless, but when we are focused on what we will become, there is an endless search for who we are.

So, what is it going to be? The choice is yours. On one hand, you can choose to go through life at the mercy of your experiences and allow your circumstances to define you. Then, when things are going well, you will experience those highs, but when things go sideways, there is no end to the depth that you might face. The reality is that all of us will experience the sometimes-cruel events of the rock tumbler. In fact, throughout our lives, many of us will share in the same circumstances as we experience things like the loss of a job, the death of a family member, the effects of broken relationships, or financial uncertainty or hardship—not to mention things that contribute to our feelings of stress, anxiety, fear, failure, or shame. At the end of the day, how we respond to whatever issue we are facing is in fact the real issue. Our response is everything, and that starts with having the right mindset toward the rock tumbler.

As we move forward, may we approach our struggles, challenges, and difficulties not as situations that we need to just "get through" or "survive" but rather as opportunities for continued growth, shaping and molding us into the best version of ourselves. ***Ready, set, let's tumble…***

V

Beyond The Rock Tumbler

PART A – THE INGREDIENTS

Lesson #1 – Your Rock

So, this is what the Sovereign Lord says: "See, I lay a stone in Zion, a tested stone, a precious cornerstone for a sure foundation; the one who trusts will never be dismayed."

Isaiah 28:16

Lesson #2 – The Other Rocks

And let us consider how we may spur one another on toward love and good deeds. Let us not give up meeting together, as some are in the habit of doing, but let us encourage one another—and all the more as you see the Day approaching.

Hebrews 10:24-25

Lesson #3 – Grit

Therefore, since we have been justified through faith, we have peace with God through our Lord Jesus Christ, through whom we have gained access by faith in this grace in which we now stand. And we rejoice in the hope of the glory of God. Not only so, but we also rejoice in our sufferings, because we know that suffering produces perseverance; perseverance, character and character, hope. And hope does not disappoint us, because God has poured out His love into our hearts by the Holy Spirit, whom He has given us.

Romans 5:1-5

Lesson #4 – Water

Jesus answered, "Everyone who drinks this water will be thirsty again, but whoever drinks the water I give him will never thirst. Indeed, the water I give him will become in him a spring of water welling up to eternal life."

John 4:13-14

PART B – THE PROCESS

Lesson #5 – Let's Get Ready to Tumble

Consider it pure joy, my brothers, whenever you face trials of many kinds, because you know that the testing of your faith develops perseverance. Perseverance must finish its work so that you may be mature and complete, not lacking anything.

James 1:2-4

Lesson #6 – Taking a Break

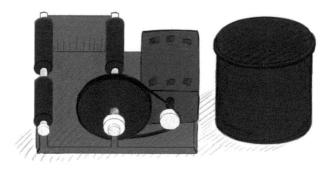

Come to me, all who are weary and burdened, and I will give you rest. Take my yoke upon you and learn from me, for I am gentle and humble in heart, and you will find rest for your souls. For my yoke is easy and my burden is light.

Matthew 11:28-30

Lesson #7 – Life Is Messy

Save me, O God, for the waters have come up to my neck. I sink in the miry depths, where there is no foothold. I have come into the deep waters; the floods engulf me. I am worn out calling for help; my throat is parched. My eyes fail, looking for my God. Those who hate me without reason outnumber the hairs on my head; many are my enemies without cause, those who seek to destroy me. I am forced to restore what I did not steal.

Psalms 69:1-4

Lesson #8 – Pulled out of the Mess

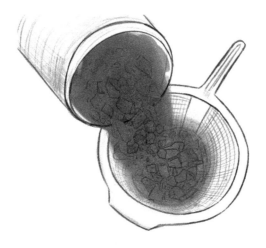

I waited patiently for the Lord; He turned to me and heard my cry. He lifted me out of the slimy pit, out of the mud and mire; he set my feet on a rock and gave me a firm place to stand.

Psalms 40:1-2

Lesson #9 – The Rinse

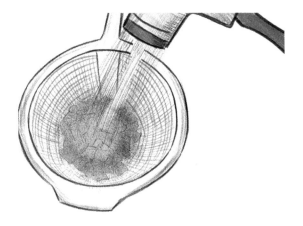

Let us draw near to God with a sincere heart in full assurance of faith, having our hearts sprinkled to cleanse us from a guilty conscience and having our bodies washed with pure water. Let us hold unswervingly to the hope we profess, for He who promised is faithful.

Hebrews 10:22-23

Lesson #10 – Deep Cleaning

Have mercy on me, O God, according to your unfailing love; according to your great compassion blot out my transgressions. Wash away all my iniquity and cleanse me from my sin…Surely you desire truth in the inner parts; you teach me wisdom in the inmost place. Cleanse me with hyssop, and I will be clean; wash me and I will be whiter than snow.

Psalms 51:1-2, 6-7

Lesson #11 – Repeat

But he said to me, "My grace is sufficient for you, for my power is made perfect in weakness." Therefore, I will boost all the more gladly about my weaknesses, so that Christ's power may rest on me. That is why, for Christ's sake, I delight in weakness, in insults, in hardships, in persecutions, in difficulties. For when I am weak, then I am strong.

2 Corinthians 12:9-10

Lesson #12 – The Process Summary

Not that I have already obtained all this, or have already been made perfect, but I press on to take hold of that for which Christ Jesus took hold of me. Brothers, I do not consider myself yet to have taken hold of it. But one thing I do: Forgetting what is behind and straining toward what is ahead, I press on toward the goal to win the prize for which God has called me heavenward in Christ Jesus.

Philippians 3:12-14

PART C – THE RESULTS

Lesson #13 – The Results Summary

Therefore, I urge you, brothers, in view of God's mercy, to offer your bodies as living sacrifices, holy and pleasing to God—this is your spiritual act of worship. Do not conform any longer to the pattern of this world, but be transformed by the renewing of your mind. Then you will be able to test and approve what God's will is—His good, pleasing and perfect will.

Romans 12:1-2

Lesson #14 – Run Your Race

Therefore, since we are surrounded by such a great cloud of witnesses, let us throw off everything that hinders and the sin that so easily entangles. And let us run with perseverance the race marked out for us.

Hebrews 12:1

Lesson #15 – Appreciating the Grind

Being confident of this, that He who has begun a good work in you will carry it on to completion until the day of Christ Jesus.

Philippians 1:6

Lesson #16 – You Are Meant to Shine

You are the light of the world. A city on a hill cannot be hidden. Neither do people light a lamp and put it under a bowl. Instead they put it on its stand, and it gives light to everyone in the house. In the same way, let your light shine before men, that they may see your good deeds and praise your Father in heaven.

Matthew 5:14-16

Acknowledgements

Family

My wife, Jennifer – Thank you for loving me. I appreciate your endless support. You have believed in me and encouraged me to chase after my purpose. You challenge me and keep me grounded. In this crazy rock tumbler of a world that we live in, I couldn't ask for a better partner. I love you.

My daughters, Shayne and Morgan – You are truly the joy of my life. I am so proud of who you are and who you are becoming. I have been honored to walk alongside you both on your journey through life. May you always be rock solid in who you are.

My parents, Bob and Jerri – You provided the foundation that made me the person I am today. Dad, you have provided an incredible living example of how to live through the rock tumbler. Growing up without a father in your life, you chose a different path for our family. You have taught me how to be a great husband

and father. Mom, you have always been the rock of our family. I am amazed by how you model a life of servant leadership and unfailing faith. Your willingness to serve others inspires me to serve as well. I appreciate your continued prayers over me and our family.

My brothers, Bryan and Robby – We certainly threw our fair share of rocks and definitely tumbled our way through childhood, at least until Mom said, "Wait until your father gets home." We also seemed to survive the knee pads and double shin guards. You have both become great husbands and loving fathers.

Professional Mentors

There have been countless mentors in my life who have poured into me over the years to help me become the person I am. From teachers to coaches and bosses, it would be impossible to mention all of them here, but I would like to acknowledge a few people who played major roles.

Jim Madrid, founder and CEO of Advance Sports Technology – You have been a mentor to me for over twenty years. I would not be where I am today without your continued support and guidance. You opened the door that allowed me to find my purpose in life. I am forever grateful for your belief in me.

Pastor David Menard and Pastor Jonathan (JC) Cooper from The Mission Church in Carlsbad, CA – You both have been tremendous resources over the years. I appreciate your spiritual leadership and guidance. You have always provided valuable insight and direction to help ensure that the content remains in the correct context.

Book Process and Previews

Patrick Gilliam, Head Coach of Women's Soccer at Trinity International University – You were one of the first people to hear the story of *The Rock Tumbler*. At that time, it was in the infant stage and not much more than an idea. You have been a great sounding board and helped provide valuable feedback throughout this process. I appreciate your time and value your friendship.

Amber Gerdes, one of the first people to read *The Rock Tumbler* – Thank you for proofreading and editing those admittedly "crummy first drafts." This book would not be possible without your insight and direction. Thank you for supporting me throughout this process.

Alex Dieringer, illustrator for *The Rock Tumbler* – Thank you for helping to bring the words and story of *The Rock Tumbler* to life. Your creativity and inspiration have taken this story to another level. I am excited to see what you will do in the future.

References

Bartholomew, Brett. *Conscious Coaching: The Art & Science of Building Buy-In*. Omaha: Brett Bartholomew, 2017.

Brown, Brene. *Dare to Lead*. New York: Penguin Random House LLC, 2018.

Clear, James. *Atomic Habits*. New York: Penguin Random House LLC, 2018.

Fessler, Leah. "'You're no genius': Her father's shut-downs made Angela Duckworth a world expert on grit." Quartz at Work, March 26, 2018. https://qz.com/work/1233940/angela-duckworth-explains-grit-is-the-key-to-success-and-self-confidence/#:~:text=As%20Duckworth%20defines%20it%2C%20grit,%2C%20years%2C%20or%20even%20decades.

Gordon, Jon. *The Power of Positive Leadership*. New Jersey: John Wiley & Sons, 2017.

Holiday, Ryan. *The Obstacle Is the Way*. New York: Penguin Group, 2014.

Merriam-Webster, s.v. "grit," accessed June 22, 2020, https://www.merriam-webster.com/dictionary/grit.

The Holy Bible, New International Version, Grand Rapids: 2002.

Sinek, Simon. *The Infinite Game*. New York: Penguin Random House LLC, 2019.

Sinek, Simon. *Leaders Eat Last: Why Some Teams Pull Together and Others Don't*. New York: Penguin Random House LLC, 2017.

Stulberg, Brad and Steve Magness. *The Passion Paradox*. New York: Rodale Books, 2019.

Stulberg, Brad and Steve Magness. *Peak Performance*. New York: Rodale Books, 2017.

Tebow, Tim. *This Is the Day*. New York: Penguin Random House LLC, 2018.

About The Author

C had Busick was born and raised in Southern California. Originally from Atascadero, CA; Chad attended California Lutheran University in Thousand Oaks. A former college soccer player, Chad graduated from Cal Lutheran with a B.S. in Psychology. Shortly after graduation, he married Jennifer and the two moved to San Diego where Chad would continue his post graduate education with classes in Sports Psychology and Counseling. Settling into North

County of San Diego, they have raised their two daughters, Shayne and Morgan.

Through his company Championship Mindset, owned with his wife Jennifer, Chad has created original content including his Championship Mindset formula and his first book, The Rock Tumbler. Chad also works closely with Jim Madrid and Advance Sports Technology. Chad's journey with AST began 20 years ago as a corporate client, where he served as a program facilitator for his previous employer. Holding a National D license with US Soccer, Chad spent 10 years incorporating the 7 Fundamentals of Mental Toughness as a competitive soccer coach in San Diego. A few years ago, he stepped away from coaching to join AST as the Director of Business Development. Chad has worked with college teams at the DI, DII, DIII and NAIA levels as well as high school and competitive teams across various sports. Chad enjoys helping players, coaches, parents and teams improve their performance and mental toughness both on and off the field. Chad is also a Power of Positive Leadership Certified Trainer with Jon Gordon Companies.

Chad be reached at:
therocktumbler.com
Chad@championshipmindset.org
Twitter: @chad_busick

About The Illustrator

Alex Dieringer is a freelance artist with about 3 years of serious illustration experience, including the upcoming release of his comic, Cursed. He has skills in traditional art mediums, as well as digital; such as Photoshop, Illustrator, and Clip Studio Paint.

CPSIA information can be obtained
at www.ICGtesting.com
Printed in the USA
LVHW021232251120
672429LV00007B/9